CBT DOODLING FOR KIDS

of related interest

Thera-Build with LEGO®
A Playful Therapeutic Approach for Promoting Emotional Well-Being in Children
Alyson Thomsen
ISBN 978 1 78592 492 7
eISBN 978 1 78450 881 4

101 Mindful Arts-Based Activities to Get Children and Adolescents Talking
Working with Severe Trauma, Abuse and Neglect Using Found and Everyday Objects
Dawn D'Amico, LCSW, PhD
ISBN 978 1 78592 731 7
eISBN 978 1 78450 422 9

Healthy Mindsets for Super Kids
A Resilience Programme for Children Aged 7–14
Stephanie Azri
Illustrated by Sid Azri
ISBN 978 1 84905 315 0
eISBN 978 0 85700 698 1

The Homunculi Approach to Social and Emotional Wellbeing
A Flexible CBT Programme for Young People on the Autism Spectrum
or with Emotional and Behavioural Difficulties
Anne Greig and Tommy MacKay
ISBN 978 1 84310 551 0
eISBN 978 0 85700 560 1

A message from author Tanja Sharpe...

Would you like to harness creativity to combat anxiety, depression and isolation in young people?
Doodling, drawing and creative expression builds bridges for young people to share their heart story without the need for words. It is a showcase of their inside world on the outside! As young people create, they make sense of what they feel and think, and this in turn boosts happy chemicals. These chemicals help to promote concentration, focus and relaxation. These exercises boost confidence, intuition and self-esteem.

Cost-effective Training at Confident Hearts
As a therapist, I work creatively with young people and I teach the adults who support them how to do the same through exercises that don't need words. The combination of therapeutic coaching, NLP, CBT and Creative Mindfulness is incredibly powerful, and I want to be able to have a greater impact globally on the young people I'm not able to reach in 1:1 work. I set up Confident Hearts with a mission to train as many people as I can to be able to inspire and empower young minds to be their most confident selves. Join our team of over 100 global coaches!

Our training is delivered to you via our professional course platform. To find out more about the training Confident Hearts offers, follow this link:

www.confidenthearts.com/jkp

CBT DOODLING FOR KIDS

50 Illustrated Handouts to Help Build Confidence and Emotional Resilience in Children Aged 6–11

TANJA SHARPE

Jessica Kingsley *Publishers*

London and Philadelphia

First published in 2019
by Jessica Kingsley Publishers
73 Collier Street
London N1 9BE, UK
and
400 Market Street, Suite 400
Philadelphia, PA 19106, USA

www.jkp.com

Copyright © Tanja Sharpe 2019

6

Library of Congress Cataloging in Publication Data
A CIP catalog record for this book is available from the Library of Congress

British Library Cataloguing in Publication Data
A CIP catalogue record for this book is available from the British Library

ISBN 978 1 78592 537 5
eISBN 978 1 78775 017 3

Printed and bound by CPI Group (UK) Ltd, Croydon, CR0 4YY

The accompanying PDF can be downloaded from www.jkp.com/voucher using the code JEAZYDE

CONTENTS

INTRODUCTION TO THIS CREATIVE CBT DOODLE THERAPY WORKBOOK

I am a qualified counsellor and mindfulness teacher to young people. I specialise in working with young people with additional needs such as autism spectrum disorder (ASD), attention deficit hyperactivity disorder (ADHD), anxiety and depression.

I noticed that there was something missing in how I delivered mindfulness style cognitive behavioural therapy (CBT) workshops and this something turned out to be creativity. I now run 'Creative Mindfulness' workshops with a CBT twist for young people, carers, parents and siblings. This has proved to be very helpful for young people who would often struggle to express emotions healthily.

This book aims to bridge the gap between CBT and mindfulness and having some time out for creative fun. The exercises in the book have been created to engage young people in exploring the story of each character and then to process what the story means for them. I have developed these characters over the last few years while working with young people; they enable them to talk about their feelings without struggling to find the words.

Each of the key methods combined within this book has its own unique set of benefits!

DOODLING

In my work with young people, I have found that doodling has helped to improve memory retention, to offer a rest for the brain when it is tired and to relieve emotional distress.

Doodling is often defined as a lot of random pictures, words and scribbles that don't make sense. In this book I refer to doodling to mean any words, pictures and scribbles which unfold within these worksheets. I am able to understand so much from a young person's doodles. What are they doodling about? Who is in the doodle? What colours are they picking and where are they using these colours within the worksheet? Our subconscious loves a creative outlet for emotional distress!

Doodling is also a great tool for problem solving. I will share an example:

I recently worked with someone who struggled to talk about a situation that they feared at school. As part of this we decided to explore the worksheets found in this book. I photocopied lots of them and laid them out on the floor. The young person chose to work with Stomper, who stomps out worries and problems. I then explored the worksheet with them using open language such as:

'What colours would you use to write down your problem and then why?'

'How does that problem make you feel in your body and where do you feel these problems?'

Without asking the direct question 'What problems are you having?' we were able to explore what was happening for the young person, in a way which enabled them to keep control over the content. This creative way of working respects the young person's right to choose and empowers them to share only what feels comfortable at that time.

CBT TOOLS FOR YOUNG PEOPLE

Cognitive behavioural therapy is known as a talking therapy which has been proven to work very effectively for young people to help them overcome conditions such as anxiety, depression, OCD and anger management. In my experience, I have found that the educational element of CBT has helped young people with ADHD and ASD to better manage some of their symptoms in a more positive, integrated and healthy way.

The aim of CBT is to challenge any patterns of behaviour and thought processes that are negative, destructive or distressing and to replace them with more positive thought patterns. It works to integrate the patterns between our thoughts, our emotions and our behaviours.

THE CBT MODEL EXPLAINED

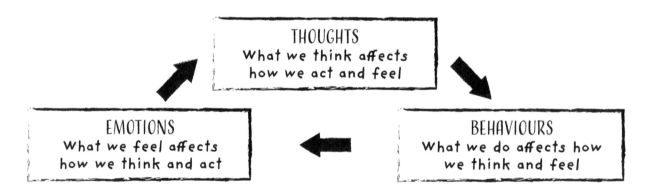

CBT is based on the theory that it is not the event or trigger which we find upsetting, but the importance and the meaning that we associate with the event. For example, two people can experience exactly the same trigger but think and feel very differently about it.

I remember running a workshop for young people where we were exploring embarrassing things that had happened at school. A group of around five identified with tripping in the classroom. Two out of the five shared how they had felt so embarrassed about the incident that they now worried about this daily, even though it had happened years before. The other three shared how they had not felt embarrassed and how it had not impacted on their confidence within school. As we unpicked this, it became clear that those who identified the incident as being life-changing and affecting their confidence had ruminating thoughts about how tripping means being 'clumsy' or even 'stupid'. When we explored this further we were able to identify where these thoughts came from and to work with these unsupportive beliefs about themselves. Those who were not affected so deeply had not previously encountered these kinds of messages around tripping in school.

It is very common for young people to start to believe their negative thoughts as being absolutely true, even when there is no evidence to support this. These beliefs can become so powerful that they change how we behave. As our behaviours deeply reinforce our thoughts, a negative cycle is started.

CBT works by recognising, reframing and releasing some of the negative beliefs that a young person has. This therapy is based on the belief that we associate negative emotions with situations and events, even when they haven't yet happened. A negative cycle then begins, as our thoughts, emotions and behaviours are all interlinked.

CBT helps young people to gain control of their thoughts, reactions and emotions by exploring beliefs, challenging assumptions, encouraging healthy and confidence-boosting 'self-talk' and identifying more positive coping strategies.

My favourite question to ask young people during a session is:

'Is it already true?'

Using this understanding and questioning allows us to explore what is simply a thought passing through and creating chaos, or what is actual fact!

CREATIVE MINDFULNESS

We have developed the first ever Creative Mindfulness programme for young people within the UK and have been running workshops and training groups to use Creative Mindfulness to increase emotional resilience in people of all ages. We love the benefits that we see when we combine creativity with mindfulness.

HOW IT WORKS

Most of us are running through life on auto-pilot. We aren't aware of how we are feeling or are experiencing life in the present moment. Illness, anxiety and depression are at an all-time high and more and more young people are developing behavioural and emotional issues. Mindfulness takes you on a journey of rediscovery and helps to integrate awareness of your body's natural rhythms, reactions and processes.

Mindfulness is described as paying more attention to the present moment – to your own thoughts and feelings, and to the world around you in a non-judgemental and compassionate way.

Mindfulness simply means awareness. Mindfulness can help you enjoy life more and understand yourself better. Mindfulness pays particular attention to your breathing, physical reactions, emotions and thoughts. It teaches you a deeper awareness of what is happening within your body and your thoughts! This is hugely beneficial when working with young people and their families.

I believe Creative Mindfulness works because the most mindful we can be is when we are focused in the moment on taking part in something creative. While we are being creative we often don't have the head space to be worrying or focusing on negative thoughts. Instead we are in the moment and focused on the activity we are taking part in. This allows us some much-needed time out and rest. It also offers an outlet for the subconscious and unconscious mind to process and share what is happening for us.

Creativity boosts our emotional wellbeing. It helps us to process our emotions and our feelings without over-thinking. Creativity helps us to integrate our senses so that we are working in tune with our body in the moment: a mindful tune in!

The main message of this book, which I always introduce to young people, is that it is not about the outcome of what we draw, doodle or create but the *process* – the space to be in the moment and to allow some freedom from thinking and judging ourselves too heavily.

ADDITIONAL GUIDANCE FOR USING THIS WORKBOOK WITH YOUNG PEOPLE

It is important to create a good working relationship with the young person you are supporting before you start to use these worksheets. A good relationship can be developed by offering trust, honesty, a non-judgemental approach, and confidentiality and by allowing young people to be autonomous and guide their own sessions.

I have found that the best way to use the worksheets is to have them photocopied and readily available for young people to choose from. You may be surprised which one a client chooses; however it is important to be client-led and to support your client to make their own choices, even when you feel there is another worksheet which may be more suitable. You just don't know what is going to unfold within the creative process.

Remember that our bodies have an innate ability to know what we need to explore and process. I believe that our unconscious and subconscious are playing a part in the process and are looking for an outlet to express. Support the creative process without influencing your client or making suggestions as this comes from your own understanding and beliefs rather than the client's.

An example that I often share involves colour work. When I first started working creatively, I supported a young person to work through anger using colours. I gave the young person a red pen to add where they most felt angry within their body and they really struggled to do this. When we explored this, my client shared that they wanted to use a green for anger and that red was one of their favourite colours. I had offered red as this was a colour that I associated with anger. By doing this I hampered the creative process and this resulted in confusion for my young client and meant that they weren't able to engage fully in a relaxed way. It is so important to remain the 'watcher' and to explore what the young person creates in front of you without judgement. This is their process!

Be open to anything that arises. Explore this with an open mind and engage fully in their process. Use open-ended questions such as:

'What colours do you feel in your body?'

Instead of:

'Do you feel pink in your heart area?'

Always keep the focus on the young person's story and point of view.

If a young person starts to engage with a worksheet and changes their mind, support them to do this without nudging them to continue. Our emotional regulatory system creates our own roadblocks and defence systems, which serve an important purpose to defend us from emotional and physical harm. Sometimes we are just not ready to process something, and this is OK!

For these worksheets to have a positive impact, it is important that the young person has chosen to engage in this process. In my experience, I have found that when I have tried to introduce worksheets to someone who isn't ready they have become quite closed or their behaviour and body language have presented as anxious.

Follow your intuition and work in a way that feels open and honest!

I hope that you find this book to be a positive addition to your creative therapy toolbox and that you enjoy using it as much as I do to enhance your work with young people!

Much love,

Tanja xx

P.S. We love to inspire people to live their most happy, healthy and fulfilling lives. If you would like to stay in touch or find out more, you can visit our website here:

www.confidenthearts.com

JOOST

Joost likes a good happiness boost. When you feel happy, you have lots more energy to spend time doing stuff that brings you joy. Share and doodle what makes you happy and remember to celebrate all that you have in your life!

HELLALAH

Hellalah loves to feel calm. When you feel calm you make lots of good chemicals in your body, which helps you to sleep, gives you good energy and makes you feel happy. Close your eyes and think of all the things that help you to feel calm. Then doodle these onto the sheet!

SNIPS

Snips loves to store happy memories. Thinking about the good stuff helps you to feel good. Think about your favourite memories and doodle them in the boxes!

LUCY

Lucy helps you to get rid of the stuff that you don't want in your life. Letting go of the stuff that makes you unhappy helps you to make space for more good stuff. Think about what you want to let go of and doodle these thoughts all around Lucy!

TERGUL

Tergul has lost her wing. Help Tergul to grow her wing
with lots of kind thoughts. Think about lots of kind
things that you can do for others. Kindness feels good.
Good feelings help Tergul to grow a new wing. Doodle
your kind thoughts and grow her a new wing!

BELLE

Belle loves to vacuum up your worries. When you give your worries to someone else, it means you have someone to help you to find a solution. Take some time to doodle your worries for Belle to vacuum away. When she does a good job, you can reward her by decorating her body. Belle loves to feel proud.

GAMALONG

Gamalong always wanted to be a superstar cloud racer. One day someone told him that he was too tall to be a superstar racer and this made him feel invisible. Then a kind star told him that if he could reach him, then he could do anything! He raced as fast as he could, and he reached the star. Now he knows that he can be anything that he wants to be! Reach for the stars and doodle your dreams!

JINKS

Jinks eats so much pie that he is starting to look like one! What do you have too much of in your life?

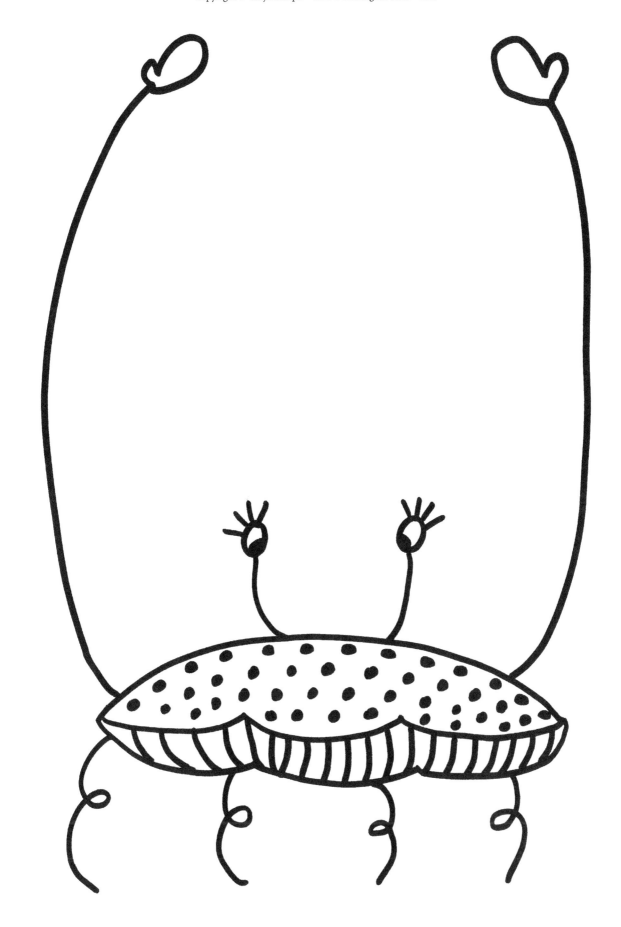

SHELBI

Shelbi likes to store your favourite important things in her safe shell. What would you like her to store for you? What is important to you?

NARLEY

Narley stresses too much and finds it hard to relax!
When he gets stressed out he feels it in his stomach
and in his heart. Where do you feel stressed out
in your body and what stresses you out?

FLODOO

Flodoo is a dream climber! He helps people to achieve their goals. Write your biggest goal in the box at the top of the mountain and then write 5 steps that you need to take to reach your goal. Colour in the mountain every time you complete another step.

TILULAH

Tilulah spends a lot of her time relaxing and listening for sounds around her. She likes to close her eyes, gently float and listen. She feels so chilled out when she does this. Can you close your eyes and listen for how many sounds you can hear around you? How many sounds can you doodle on to this sheet?

DUDDILS

Duddils is shy and hides away when he has to meet new people or go to new places. He doesn't like to try new things. Are there some things that you would like to try? How will you feel when you try new things and achieve them? Doodle them here!

SKANDOOL

Skandool is unique and rare! She has the longest neck in the tribe. When she was younger she used to be teased about this. Now she can reach the tastiest fruit in the trees and everyone asks her for help. Celebrate how unique you are! Doodle what makes you different to other people!

SQUIPS

Squips is really good at loving herself! When you love yourself, you grow lots of good chemicals in your body, which helps you to feel happy, healthy and strong! Can you say this... 'I am awesome and unique' and give yourself a hug?

PEPTWI

Peptwi is a magic spy glass and likes to show you the things that you most want to see. Doodle something, someone or some place that you want to see in Peptwi!

TRAV

Trav is a magic carpet and wants to take you on a journey. If you could go anywhere, where would you go and who would you take with you?

RAE

Rae like to help you to celebrate all the things that make you awesome! Can you doodle something that makes you awesome in each of these 12 rays?

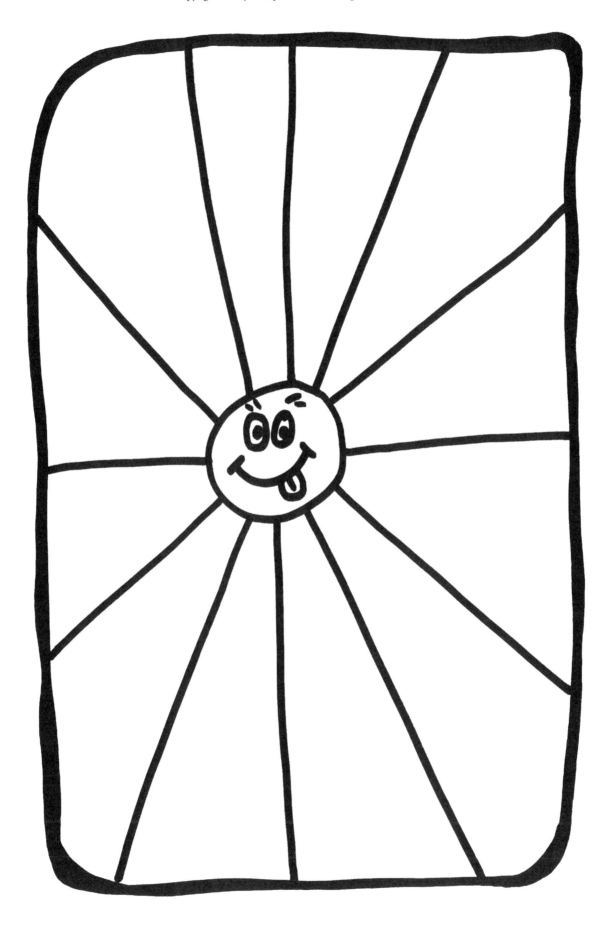

STOMPER

Stomper has huge feet and he likes to use these to stomp out any worries and problems that you need help with. Doodle as many things as you can and give him permission to stomp these out for you!

YOUR TRIBE

Your tribe is waiting to be doodled from your imagination. Doodle a tribe of characters! Give them names and magic powers! What will you create?

TINKS

Tinks is hiding a magic gift for you!
What do you think or hope that it might be?
Doodle your hopes and ideas here!

BERRI

Berri loves a party. She loves to plan for her perfect party by doodling and using her imagination. If you were planning your perfect party, what would you plan? Who would be there, where would it be and what would it be like? You could have it anywhere in the world and invite anyone that you want!

INVENTIOUS

You guessed it (probably)! Inventious loves to invent! He has run out of ideas though! If you could invent something, what would it be and what would it do?

DOOPSDIE

Doopsdie often feels sad and needs some help to doodle her feelings. What makes you feel sad and what ways can you think of to start to feel better again? Doodle as many as you can!

ANGEL

Angel is a gratitude flower and loves nothing more than
to read and hear all of our thankful and grateful thoughts.
When we are grateful, her petals become brighter and
she feels so much shinier and happier. Can you doodle
as many happy thoughts as you can think of?

FRENDZ

These frendz are best friends and they trust each
other so much! Who do you trust in your life and why
do you trust them? Doodle your thoughts here!

TILLS

Tills likes to feel proud. She shares this feeling with other people by sending happy positive vibes out into the world with her kind, proud thoughts. What do you feel proud of? Doodle your thoughts here!

PEG

Peg loves to read but has run out of books. He really wants to read your life story. Can you create a book cover for your life? What title would you give a book about your life, who would be the characters and what would your life be like? Doodle this! Peg is so excited to see what you write!

JUNIPA

Junipa grants your wishes using her magical head wands!
How many wishes do you have? What would you wish for?
What would you wish for that doesn't cost any money?

FLOW

Flow likes to have lots of colour. Somehow an invisibility spell was cast in her ocean and she has lost all of her colour, so isn't feeling very well. Can you give her back some colour and create a beautiful ocean for her to swim in?

SONAR

Sonar is a healer and lifts other people's moods by sending out positive healing vibes to everyone around her. If you rub her stomach, then she will send you some healing vibes too. What do you need help with right now?

THE BALLOO BROTHERS

Tam, Moo, Doodle and Bingo are brothers. They float around waiting to take your worries far, far, away. What is worrying you right now? Would you like to doodle these in the balloons and ask the Balloo Brothers to take them away?

YOUR DAY AS A COMIC

Sometimes it can be hard to talk about your problems with other people. Sometimes it is easier to doodle these instead. Can you create a comic story about your day?

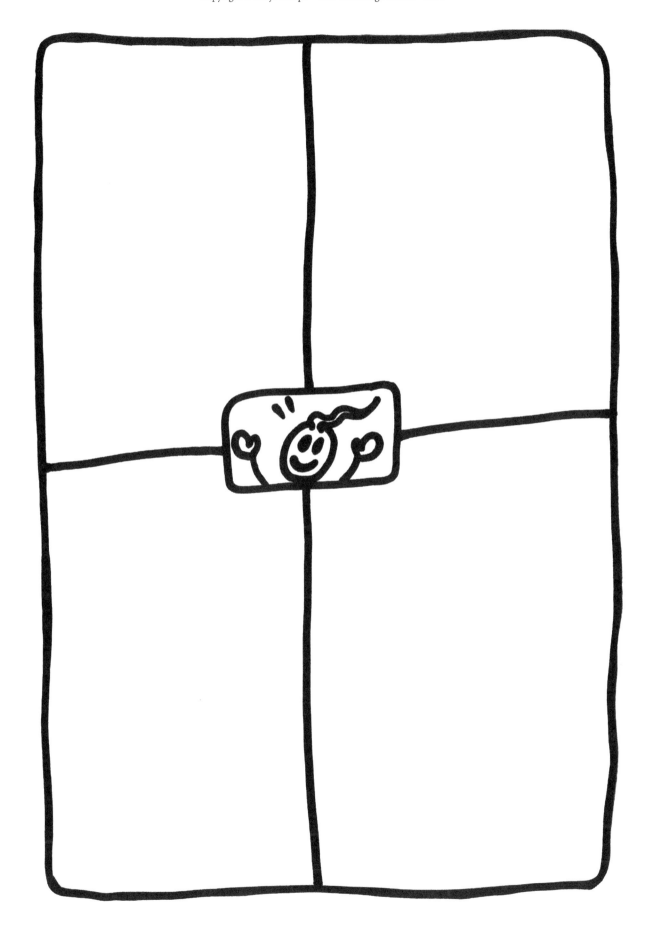

BOOPS

Boops really hates it when people tease him or push his buttons. This makes him feel really angry! What pushes your buttons? Can you doodle a button for each annoying thing?

TINGA

Tinga loves to explore and create new island homes. He has landed here and wants your help! If you landed on an island and could create a new awesome home, what would you create? Who would be with you and what would it look like? What would you need and take with you?

BONGIL

Bongil has magic gifts. He can fly, choose to be invisible and grant wishes! He is also kind, helpful, creative and energetic. What magical gifts do you have and offer the world around you?

SEEYA

Seeya is going on a journey to find her ultimate treasure. This kind of treasure doesn't cost money – health, happiness, friendships, sleep, love and energy. Ultimate treasure is good for us and good for others too! What would be your ultimate treasure and how can you find it? Create your own timeline treasure map! Doodle all of the ways that you can create more of your ultimate treasure in your life.

KAYA

Kaya cares a lot about forgiveness. She knows that when we can forgive people it helps us to feel much happier and healthier in our own lives. Who do you want to forgive? Doodle it on the sheet. Ask for help if you need it and when you are ready, close your eyes, send forgiveness and clap three times.

SPLOG

Splog is a walking blog. She likes to talk about friendships. She would like you to help her to write a recipe for what makes a good friend. Can you help her and doodle a list of what you think makes a good friend?

ROX

Rox is a stinger! You know when he gets angry because of his body language. He has long stingers which look worse than they actually are. He likes to keep people away. What he really needs is help to come up with some ideas about how to be less angry. Can you help him by sharing what makes you angry and how you help yourself to calm down?

BIGZ

Bigz is a super cool listener. Do you have anything that you want to tell someone? You can doodle anything on this sheet!

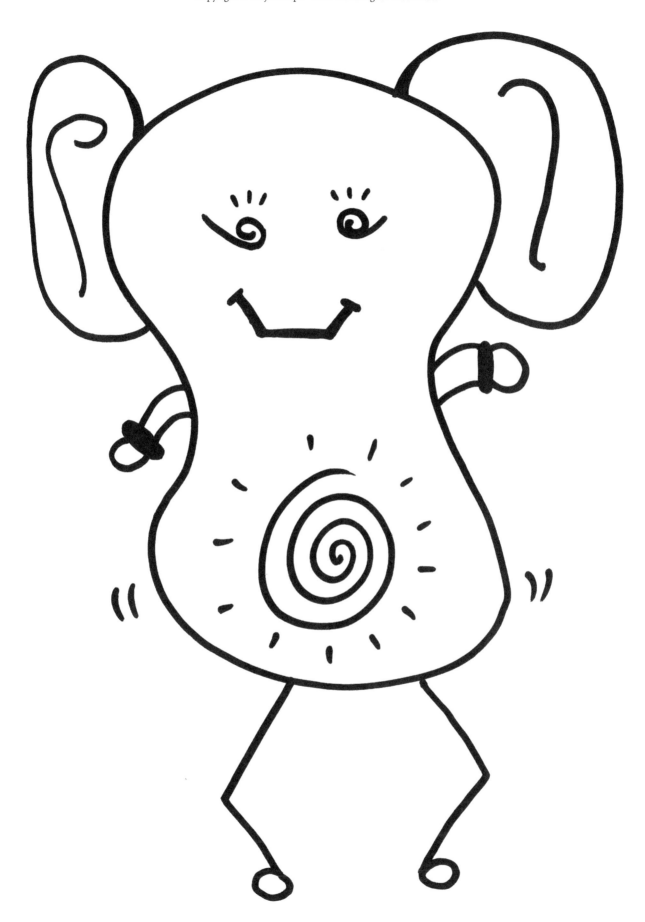

JUDD

Judd likes to challenge himself. He knows that anything is possible when you say so and you believe it. Recently, he won a tightrope walking contest when everyone else said that he couldn't do it. Is there something that you would like to do that feels impossible right now? Doodle that here and write down 3 big reasons why it is possible!

AMIE

Amie is stubborn and spiky. She is feeling upset because she didn't apologise to her friend even though she knew she was wrong. Now she misses her friend. Can you doodle as many ways that you can think of to help her to say sorry to her friend?

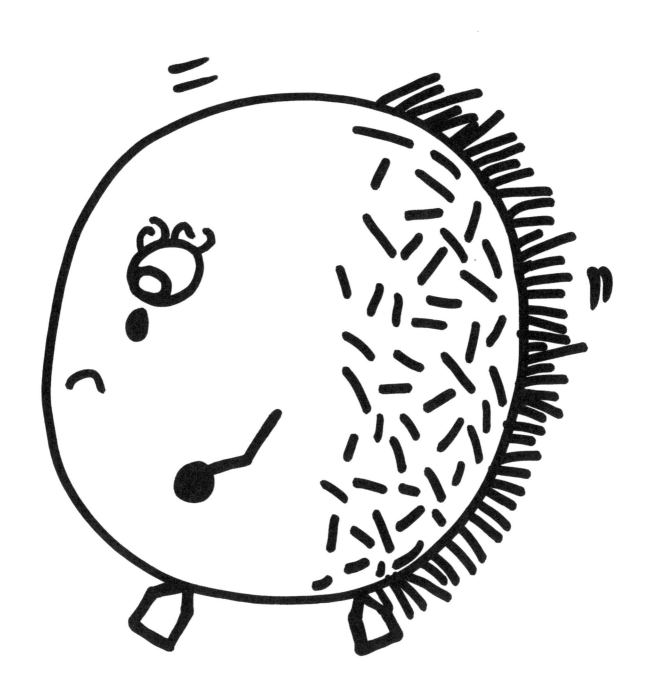

THE CLOUDS

The Clouds love to take care of each other. They are a family and help each other to keep the rain system working. Who is in your family and how do you all help each other out? Do you need to doodle more clouds?

ROOTZ

Rootz is a magic tree. He helps you to discover lots of hidden things about yourself. The top of the tree is what you show to the world around you. The bottom of the tree, the roots, is what people don't get to see about you! Can you write or doodle as many things about you that people don't know? Can you doodle and finish the top of the tree to show what people do know about you?

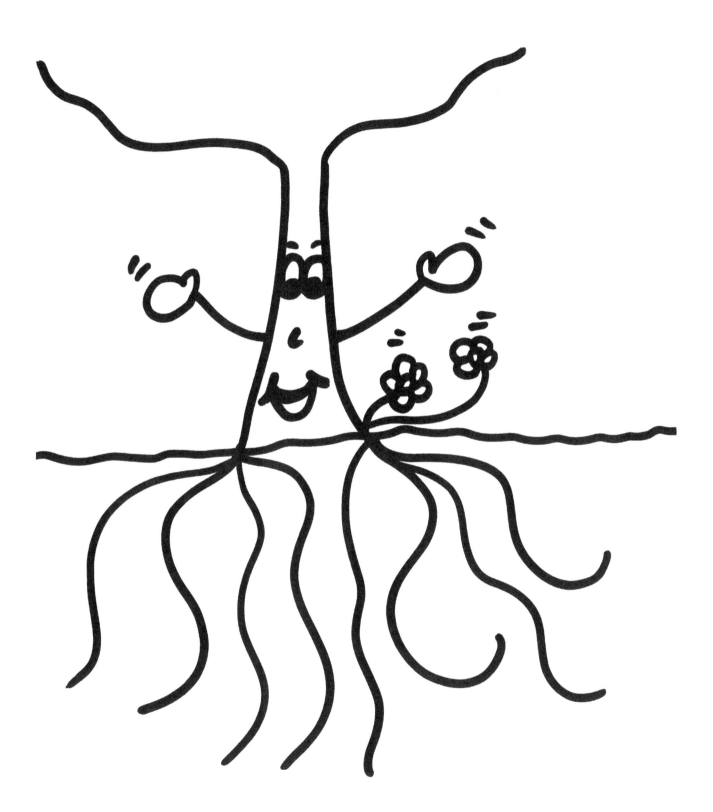

KRISP

Krisp is a dream storer. He stores your dreams so that you can remember them. Can you remember your dreams and doodle them into the memory clouds?

TEELE

Teele loves to be mindful! She likes to focus on her breathing to help her to relax. She likes to close her eyes and breathe into her stomach, filling it with fresh air. She likes to breathe out and imagine that all of her worries and any stress are leaving her body! Would you like to breathe with Teele? Could you add some colour to her picture every time you breathe out?

SUPER STAR THOUGHTS

The Super Stars often get their thoughts tangled up in their heads. They struggle to make sense of it all and start to feel stressed. Do you ever feel like this? Write the thoughts that you have right now on this sheet and let's see if you can untangle your thoughts! Circle the thoughts that make you feel unhappy. Then circle the thoughts that help you to feel happy in a different colour. Cross out the unhappy thoughts and imagine them disappearing. Colour in your happy thoughts and celebrate what an awesome superstar you are!

DANCAR

Dancar is a tree dancer. To be a tree dancer you have to have energy and keep yourself healthy. He makes sure that he gets lots of sleep, drinks water, eats fruit and vegetables and spends time in nature. He loves it when it rains, when the winds blow and when the sun shines. What do you need more of to keep yourself healthy?

EM

Em takes care of nature and the earth as she knows that the earth takes care of her. She likes to recycle, water plants, grow things, make homes for the bugs in her garden, put water out for the birds in the hot weather and take care of bees. She knows that the bees help our food to grow and the trees help us to breathe. What can you do more of to help nature?